Bass 1

INTRODUCTION

W9-BLU-278

DISCARD

You bought a bass...so now what?

Congratulations! You look great holding that new bass (even standing in front of the mirror, lip-synching to the radio, swinging your hips back and forth). But won't your friends and family be even more impressed if you can actually play the darn thing?

In just a couple of weeks, we'll have you playing some very well-known tunes, as well as jamming on some new ones. By the end of this book, it's on to the hits—The Beatles, Clapton, Hendrix, and more.

All we ask is that you observe the three Ps: **patience, practice** and **pace yourself.**

Don't try to bite off more than you can chew, and DON'T skip ahead. If your fingers hurt, take the day off. If you get frustrated, put it down and come back later. If you forget something, go back and learn it again. If you're having a great time, forget about dinner and keep on playing. Most importantly, have fun!

ABOUT THE CD

(...no, it's not a coaster!)

Glad you noticed the added bonus—a CD! Each music example in the book is included on the CD, so you can hear how it sounds and play along when you're ready. Take a listen whenever you see this symbol: **❶**

Each example on the CD is preceded by one measure of "clicks" to indicate the tempo and meter. Pan right to hear the bass part emphasized. Pan left to hear the accompaniment emphasized. As you become more confident, try playing the bass part along with the rest of the "band."

HAL•LEONARD® CORPORATION

7777 W. BLUEMOUND RD. P.O. BOX 13819 MILWAUKEE, WI 53213

Visit Hal Leonard on the internet at http: // www.halleonard.com

A GOOD PLACE TO START

Your bass is your friend...

An instrument can be like a good friend through the years—get you through the rough times and help you sing away the blues. So, before we get started, give your new four-stringed friend a name.

What a beauty!

Below is a standard electric bass. Get acquainted with the parts of your bass, and don't forget to give it a name.

head

tuning keys

nut

neck

frets

fingerboard

position markers

body

pickups

tone/volume controls

output jack

bridge

TUNING

When you tune, you correct the pitch of each string. **Pitch** means how high or low a musical tone is. This is adjusted by tightening (or loosening) the string, using the tuning keys on the head of the bass. The tighter the string, the higher the pitch.

Your four strings should be tuned to these pitches (low to high): **E-A-D-G.**

CAUTION: Tighten slowly and not too much, or you'll be heading back to the store to buy new strings!

Piano tuning

No, you aren't about to tune an entire piano! If you have a piano or electric keyboard nearby, play the above notes one at a time and tune the corresponding string until its pitch matches that of the piano.

Electronic tuner

If you don't have the luxury of a piano or keyboard, you may want to purchase an electronic tuner.

A tuner will "listen" to each string as you play it and indicate whether the pitch is too high or too low.

Don't give up hope—If you don't have a piano and you can't buy a tuner, there's yet another solution...

Relative tuning

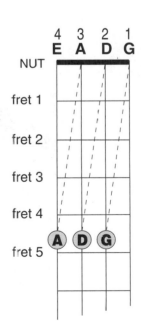

To tune your bass by ear, you must tune the strings to each other. This is done in the following manner:

 Assuming string 4 is already E, press string 4 behind fret 5, play the depressed string 4 and open string 3 together. When the two sounds match, you're in tune.

 Press string 3 behind fret 5 and tune open string 2 to it.

 Press string 2 behind fret 5 and tune open string 1 to it.

A FEW MORE THINGS

(...before we jam!)

Sit down and stay a while...

Perhaps the most comfortable and least tiring way to learn bass is to sit while playing.

Once you learn a few tunes, feel free to stand up, lay down, hold it behind your head, or whatever. But for now let's put that extra effort to better use—playing.

sitting

standing

Please hold...

Hold the neck of the bass with your **left hand**, with your thumb resting comfortably behind the neck.

Hold the neck slightly upwards—not downwards (at least not until you're on stage in front of thousands of fans).

left hand position (fingers)

left hand position (thumb)

There's nothing stressful here, so don't grip the neck too hard (you might strangle it!).

Picture This...

Fingerboard diagrams (or "grids") picture a portion of the fretboard and show you where to play the notes and chords. Circles are drawn onto the diagram to indicate the notes being played.

Think of your fingers as being numbered 1 through 4.

fold

DOG-EAR THESE TWO PAGES
(...you'll need to review them later)

Music is a language with its own symbols, structure, and rules (and exceptions to those rules). To read, write, and play music requires knowing all the symbols and rules. But let's take it one step at a time (a few now, a few later)...

Notes

Music is written with little doo-hickeys called **notes.** Notes come in all shapes and sizes. A note has two essential characteristics: **pitch** (indicated by its position on the staff) and **rhythmic value** (indicated by the following symbols):

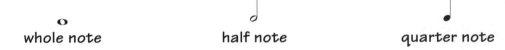

whole note   half note   quarter note

The rhythmic value lets you know how many beats the note lasts. Most commonly, a quarter note equals one beat. After that it's just like fractions (we hate math, too!):

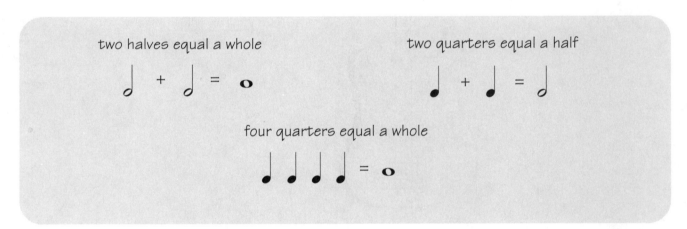

two halves equal a whole   two quarters equal a half

four quarters equal a whole

Staff and Clef

All the notes are written on (or nearby) a **staff,** which consists of five parallel lines and four spaces. Each line and space represents a different pitch. A symbol called a **clef** indicates which pitches are represented.

bass clef →
F   G   A   B   C   D   E   F   G   A   B

Ledger Lines

Since not all notes will fit on just five lines and four spaces, **ledger lines** are used to extend the staff:

E   C   D   E

Measures (or Bars)

Notes on a staff are divided into **measures** (or "bars") to help you keep track of where you are in the song.

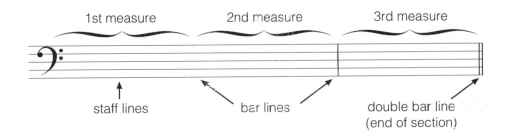

Time Signatures (or Meters)

A **time signature** (or "meter") indicates how many beats will appear in each measure. It contains two numbers: the top number tells you how many beats will be in each measure; the bottom number says what type of note will equal one beat.

Tablature

Tablature (or "TAB") is a specially designed staff for bassists. The four lines on a tablature staff represent (you guessed it!) the four strings on your bass. A number is placed on a line to indicate which fret to press.

IMPORTANT: Tablature should be used simply as a guide. You should still observe the notes, time signatures, and rhythmic values written on the music staff.

By the way, all of the music examples in this book use both a staff and tablature to make life easier (you're welcome!).

☞   **R**elax for a while, read through it again later, and then move on.
         (Trust us—as we go through the book, you'll start to understand it.)

7

LESSON 1
Don't just sit there, play something!

If the left hand "selects" a note by depressing a string at a fret, what does the **right hand** do? The right hand actually plays the strings, but you have three choices of how to play with the right hand:

1. With a pick...

Because of its more accented sound, this is a preferred method of playing by many rock bass players. Hold the pick in your right hand, as shown, and attack each string:

Pick with **downstrokes** (attack in a downward motion) or **upstrokes** (attack in an upward motion).

Using all downstrokes, play four beats on each open string (meaning don't press any frets) with your pick:

◆2 Picking and Grinning

Try the same example again but use upstrokes.

2. Fingerstyle playing...

This is the traditional way of playing and allows you more control (since your fingers can feel where to go). Rest your thumb on the **pickup** and play the strings with finger 1 (your index finger).

After you play a string, let finger 1 rest on the next string up. For example, play string 3 and rest finger 1 against string 4.

IMPORTANT: Don't let your right-hand fingers "curl up." Notice the relaxed position in the photo above.

◆3 Fingerstyle Practice

NOTE: After playing string 4, you can rest finger 1 against the body of the bass.

3. Alternate fingers...

A third (and faster) way to play is to alternate between fingers 1 and 2. Keep your hand in fingerstyle position (thumb resting on the pickup) and play string 3 once with finger 1, then once with finger 2:

◆4 Two-Finger Jam

YOUR CHOICE: Choose the right-hand playing style that's the most comfortable and best-sounding to you.

LESSON 2
G, this is easy...

You've chosen a playing style. You know all the open strings. And you're eager to play. Let's get down to business...

String 1: G

Forget strings 2-4; let's concentrate on string 1 for now. Use the photos and fingerboard diagrams below to play your new note A.

You just learned it, but it's worth repeating. Here's the open string G:

G

Play string 1 while pressing fret 2 with finger 2 and you hear A, which lies just above G on the staff:

A

Practice your new notes. (If you need a quick review of rhythmic values or time signatures, flip back to page 6.)

◆5 Two-Note Jam

☞ "What happened to fret 1?" That note is A-flat. We'll explain **flats** later.

NOTE: We realize that you already learned another A (open string 3 on page 8). But since the musical alphabet consists of only the letters A-G, this type of repetition will eventually occur with all notes.

Play string 3 open, followed by your new A:

◆6 Same Name, Different Note

Sound similar? The new A sounds one **octave** higher than string 3. An octave means eight notes apart. Bass players play lots of octaves, so get used to this new concept.

Put it to good use...

Just like reading a book, you should be going to the next line in the song as soon as you reach the end of each staff. However, when you see this symbol ( ), you are at the end of that song.

◆7 My Sharocka!

11

SOME MORE NOTES ON MUSIC
(...pardon the pun!)

Before going to Lesson 3, we want to tell you some more about the hieroglyphics of music.

Rests...

A musical **rest** is a pause. Rests are like notes in that they have their own rhythmic values, instructing the musician how long (or how many beats) to pause:

whole rest
(four beats)

half rest
(two beats)

quarter rest
(one beat)

IMPORTANT: A rest does not mean rest your fingers or put your bass down! During a rest you should get your fingers into position for the next set of notes.

◆8 Take a Load Off

PLAYING TIP: During a rest, practice **muting** the strings with your left hand (so there is no sound).

◆9 Rock, Roll, and Rest

LESSON 3
Moving on...

Take a few seconds, flip back to page 3 and make sure your bass is still in tune. (If the mirror breaks, it probably isn't!)

String 2: D

  A quick reminder of open string D:

D

  Now play string 2 while pressing fret 2 with finger 2 and you get E:

E

  Press fret 3 with finger 3 and hear F:

F

Time for another workout. (Practice slowly and count out loud!)

10 D-E-F

When you feel comfortable with D-E-F, try them in combination with your other two notes...

CHANGING STRINGS: When changing fingers from string 1 to string 2, try to let your eyes move ahead in the music, and your finger move to the correct string before the next note occurs.

⑪ DEF Jam

HELPFUL HINT: When playing a higher note, leave the lower note depressed. For example, leave finger 2 on E while pressing finger 3 on F. When you go back to E, simply lift finger 3.

⑫ Bass Boogie

☞ Repeat these examples at least twice more, playing a bit faster each time.
When you're ready (and after a snack from the 'fridge), we'll move on to Lesson 4.

LESSON 4
Three's company...

Unbelievable—six notes already. You're a fast learner! How 'bout another string? (Make sure you're still in tune, if not—page 3.)

String 3: A

String 3 is exactly like string 2 (except it's thicker):

  Don't forget the open string is A:

A

 Press fret 2 with finger 2 and you get B. (Keep those fingers arched!):

B

  Press fret 3 with finger 3. That's C:

C

Can you feel a practice tune coming?

🔷13 A-B-C Rock

Now play all the notes you've learned...

A to A

Do you realize what you just played? That was your first musical **scale**—A minor!

What's a musical scale?

Scales are arrangements of notes in specific patterns of **half steps** (one fret apart) and **whole steps** (two frets apart). Most scales have eight notes with the top and bottom notes being an octave apart. The one you just played started on A and used a **minor pattern**, thus it was the A minor scale.

Try this bass line that's built on the A minor scale...

Rockin' Riff

Scales are essential to bass players! They're the basis for all your riffs and licks. We'll learn many more scales throughout this book, but for now...

YOU GOT RHYTHM

Nice tie!

A **tie** connects two notes and tells you to hold the first note through to the end of the tied note:

Simple Simon! Try some bass lines with ties and dots...

The ones with dots are nice, too!

Another way to extend the value of a note is to use a **dot**. A dot extends the note by one-half of its value. Most common is the **dotted half** note:

Simple Simon! Try some bass lines with ties and dots...

16 Extend This!

Remember to count out loud until you begin to think and feel the beat.

CAREFUL! The next one is in 3/4 meter. That is, there are three beats per measure. (For a quick review, flip back to page 7.)

◆17 Rockin' in Three

Back to 4/4 meter (or four beats per measure)...

◆18 Fit to Be Tied

Excellent! But can you do it faster? Are you playing along with the CD?

19 Crosswalk Blues

Repeat signs have two dots before or after a double bar line ( ). They simply tell you to (you guessed it!) repeat everything in between. If only one sign appears ( ), repeat from the beginning of the piece.

20 Good Team Spirit

☞ This is a good time to take a break, maybe get some ice cream.
Then come back, review Lessons 1-4 again and continue with Lesson 5.

LESSON 5
A little bit lower now...

Let's check your progress: three strings and nine notes. It's like eating chips—just can't stop, can you? Well then, let's tackle another string...

String 4: E

This time you get to play fret 1 and skip fret 2 (we'll explain why in the next lesson)...

Of course, open string 4 is E:

Wake up finger 1, press fret 1, and you get low F (your second F, so far):

Skip fret 2 and press fret 3 with finger 3 (careful, it's a stretch!). That's low G:

Turn it up and let's rock with these new low notes...

21 E-F-G

Just for kicks, play it two more times.

20

Remember the A-A octave? Now you know four octave pairs. (We shouldn't have to tell you where they are!)

22 Octaves Apart

☞ COOL THING TO KNOW: You can quickly find the octave from any note simply by moving two frets up and two strings over.

23 (Not So) Giant Leaps

If your fingertips hurt, take a break. But never fear—the more you practice, the faster they will toughen up. (Hey, no pain...no gain.)

YOU STILL GOT RHYTHM

Can you spare a quarter? How 'bout an eighth?

An eighth note has a flag on it: ♪

Two eighth notes equal one quarter note (or one beat in 4/4 and 3/4). To make it easier on the eyes (you're welcome), eighth notes are connected with a **beam**:

To count eighth notes, divide the beat into two and use "and" between the beats:

1   (&)   2   (&)   3   &   4   &

Practice this by first counting out loud while tapping your foot on the beat, then play the notes while counting and tapping:

1 (&) 2 (&) 3 & 4 (&)   1 & 2 & 3 (&) 4 (&)

What about the rest? ♪

Eighth rests are the same, but you...pause. Count, tap, play, and pause with the following:

1 (&) 2 (& 3) & 4 (&)   1 & 2 (&) 3 & (4) &

Now try a bass line with eighth notes. (Keep that foot going!)

24 Eighth Note Rockin'

Excellent. But don't stop there...

Pickups aren't just trucks...

Instead of starting a song with rests, a **pickup measure** may be used. A pickup measure simply deletes the rests. So, if a pickup has only one beat, you count "1, 2, 3" and start playing on beat 4:

Try these riffs with pickup measures:

◆25 Pickup and Jam

Watch out for the eighth-note pickup in the next song, and remember to mute the strings during the rests...

◆26 Sneakin' Around

Remember to practice slowly! Speed up the tempo only as you become more familiar with the notes.

23

LESSON 6

You look sharp!

Why we skipped those frets...

As we learned on page 16, music is made up of **half steps** and **whole steps**. When a song requires a note to be only a half step higher or lower, a symbol is placed by that note.

One half step higher is called a **sharp** and looks like a tic-tac-toe board: ♯

One half-step lower is called a **flat** and looks like a backwards note with no air in it: ♭

EXCEPTION TO THE RULE: From E to F is only a half step; from B to C is only a half step. (Look at the white keys on the piano diagram on page 3.)

We'll learn two notes we skipped earlier—a sharp and a flat:

  On string 4, press fret 2 with finger 2 and play F-sharp:

  On string 3, press fret 1 with finger 1 and play B-flat:

27 *Groovin'*

◆28 Sharpening Groove

As promised, here's another "sharp-locking" (couldn't resist!) scale:

◆29 E Minor Scale

Repeat the scale again and then try a riff based on it (careful, the riff is in 3/4 and has all eighth notes):

◆30 E Minor Riff

Wow, those fingers can really move! ("Wow, those fingers can really tangle!") Practice and practice some more.

Now for another scale—one that uses the flat you learned:

31 F Major Scale

Congratulations! That was your first **major** scale (we'll explain later). Try a groove and a song based on the F major scale:

32 Unscaling F

NEW RULE: A **natural sign** (♮) cancels a sharp or flat on a note, returning it to its natural pitch (but only within that measure).

33 Heartbroken

What's in a Name?

Two things give a scale its name: the scale's lowest note (called the **root** note) and the **pattern** of whole steps and half steps used. (For a review of steps, flip back to page 16.)

Major vs. minor...

As you can see (and hear), a major scale is no bigger (or any more important) than a minor one, it's just a name. The real difference between the two is the specific pattern of half steps and whole steps used to create the scale. These patterns can be used to build scales on any note.

Here's are illustrations of the major and minor scale patterns:

34 Major Scale Pattern

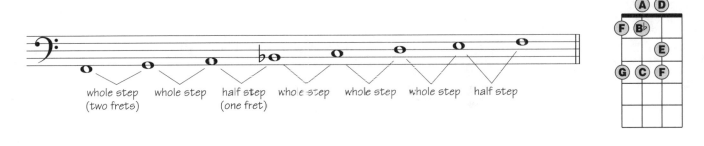

whole step (two frets)   whole step   half step (one fret)   whole step   whole step   whole step   half step

35 Minor Scale Pattern

whole step   half step   whole step   whole step   half step   whole step   whole step

LEARN IT BY EAR: Without checking the pattern, you can hear the difference between a major and minor scale.
Put simply, a major scale sounds "happy;" a minor scale sounds "sad."

LESSON 7
Almost forgot...

You want more notes? Here are two more notes we skipped on fret 1 earlier...

Notes: E-flat and A-flat

On string 2, press fret 1 with finger 1 and play E-flat:

E♭

On string 1, press fret 1 with finger 1 and play A-flat:

A♭

36 More Rock 'n' Roll

Connect the dots...

Remember the dotted half note (three beats)? A **dotted quarter** note gets one and a half beats:

quarter note   +   dot   =   dotted quarter note
(1 beat)   (1/2 beat)   (1 1/2 beats)

Think of it as being like a quarter note tied to an eighth note.

Listen to the next two examples on the CD while you clap the beat. Once you can feel the rhythm of the dotted quarter, try playing it...

37 Ballad Style

38 Dusty Road

This was a short lesson, but DON'T RUSH! Take your time and review it again (and again, and again)...

LESSON 8

It's in your roots...

As you learned, the **root note** is the lowest note of a scale, and the note that names the scale. Roots also name **chords**...

What's a chord?

Chords consist of three or more notes played simultaneously. **Chord symbols** (like the ones below) are written above the staff, indicating which chords are being played in each measure.

Listen to some examples of chords on the CD:

39 G–Em–C–D–G

Accompanying chords...

Although bass players don't normally play chords, it's essential to know about them, since your bass lines will use the notes of the chord being played.

Play track 39 on the CD again. For the next song, you'll play the root note of each chord symbol...

40 Rootin' Around

Try varying the accompaniment rhythm on the same type of song.

41 Rhythmically Rootin' Around

A bit faster now...

◈42 Some Fast Rootin'

Here are several more examples of root note accompaniment. Just follow the chord symbols...

◈43 Punk Groove

◈44 Heavy Rock Groove #1

◈45 Heavy Rock Groove #2

In addition to the root note, you can use other notes of the scale to create your bass lines...

Octave...

Interchange the root note with an octave higher or lower...

46 Jumpin' Bass

Go slowly at first! Remember the three Ps: patience, practice, and pace yourself.

47 Hard Rocktaves

48 When Johnny Comes Rockin' Home

Fifth...

Remember the major scale pattern? (If not, flip back to page 27.) Five notes up the scale is the **fifth** (makes sense, huh?).

Chords also have fifths. Simply count the root note of a chord as "1" and go up the scale to "5" to find any chord's fifth.

Interchange the root note with the fifth for a really cool sounding bass line:

49 A Fifth of Bass

☞ COOL THING TO KNOW: A fifth above any note is always two frets up and one string over.

50 Auld Lang Syne

You can also play the fifth **below** the chord's root. For example, C's fifth is G. You can play G above C, or G below C:

☞ COOL THING TO KNOW: The easy part of playing the fifth below the root is that it's on the same fret as the root (only it's one string lower):

51 Pop Punk

52 Greensleeves

Try mixing roots, fifths, and octaves (and a few notes in between)...

53 Rock Groove

Remember to watch the music, NOT your fingers!

54 Scarborough Fair

WARNING: Continuing without sleep could be detrimental
to your further enjoyment of the bass.
Take a long break and get some sleep!

LESSON 9
How high can you go?

Are you still in tune? Relaxed? Ready for even more notes?

Notes on fret 4

Wake up finger 4 (yeah you, pinkie!) and stretch it up to fret 4 on each string to learn the following new notes:

On string 1, fret 4 is "high B":

B

On string 2, fret 4 is F-sharp (your second F-sharp):

F#

String 3, fret 4 is C-sharp:

C#

String 4, fret 4 is G-sharp:

G#

◆55 Fourth Fret Jam

36

56 Rockin' Sharps

Bassists never die, they just go out of tune. (Make sure you're not!)

57 Private Eye Groove

If you're going to play up high for a while, you can do so without stretching poor ol' finger 4...

Second Position

Slide your hand up the neck of your bass so that finger 1 is positioned at fret 2. On string 1, finger 1 now plays A, finger 3 plays "high B" and finger 4 learns a new note...

Fret 5 is "high C," written on one ledger line above the staff:

C

Now try out your new note (in second position)...

58 High C Shuffle

NOTE: fret 5 on the other three strings is the same note as the next open string. Depending on the nature of the song, you can choose whether to play these three notes on an open string or fret 5. (Options are nice, huh?)

Here is yet another major scale with your new "high C":

59 C Major Scale

YOU GOT THE BLUES

Another scale pattern that you'll be glad we taught you is the **blues scale**. Listen on the CD, then try playing a blues scale with C as the root note:

60 Blues Scale Pattern

whole step · half step · whole step · half step · half step · one and a half steps (three frets) · whole step

Commit this scale pattern to memory! Use the pattern, or just parts of it, to create some excellent-sounding riffs on any root note...

61 Funky Blues

62 Fast Blues

LESSON 10

Keys, please...

A song based on the C major scale is in the **key** of C. Since the C major scale has no sharps or flats, songs and riffs in the key of C also have no sharps or flats:

63 Heartland Rock

Similarly, songs in the key of G are based on the G major scale, which has one sharp—the F-sharp you learned on string 2, fret 4:

64 G Major Scale

FINGERING TIP: Instead of stretching, try the scale again with your hand in second position (ah, much more comfortable!). You'll also find it easier to use second position to play riffs in the key of G.

40

Rather than have a symbol by every sharp in a song, a **key signature** can be used at the beginning of each line to indicate which notes are sharp throughout the song. For example, the key of G has one sharp, so its key signature will have a sharp on the F-line, telling you to play all Fs as F-sharp.

The next tune's in the key of G (notice the key signature), so use second position for ease and comfort:

65 Rockin' in G

No key signature means (you guessed it!) the key of C:

66 Worried Blues

So, if no key signature means the key of C and one sharp means the key of G, how 'bout a key signature with one flat? That's the key of F, based on the F major scale (back on page 26)...

67 Rockin' Up the Board

HELPFUL HINT: Let your eyes read ahead of the note that you're actually playing (yeah, easy for us to say?!).

68 Good Night, My Fans

CAUTION: You are nearing the end of this book.
Take a break, run to your local music dealer, and buy **FastTrack Bass Songbook!**
(You'll be glad you did.)

EVERYTHING AND THE KITCHEN SYNC...

Finally, let us tell you about one of the most essential (and fun) rhythmic concepts in music...

Syncopation

Syncopation is simply playing notes "off the beat." It makes the music sound less predictable (and, hey, it's great to dance to). Listen to a non-sycopated example on the CD:

69 Not Quite

Now, listen to the same example with syncopation:

70 Just Right

You can still feel the beat, but it certainly has a hipper groove to it.

Try playing this bass line with syncopation. Stress the notes that have an **accent** mark ">" above them (most of which will not be on the downbeat)...

71 In Sync

LESSON 11

Time to charge admission...

This isn't really a Lesson...it's a jam session! All the FastTrack books (Guitar, Keyboard, Bass, and Drums) have the same last section. This way, you can either play by yourself along with the CD or form a band with your friends.

So, whether the band's on the CD or in your garage, let the show begin...

🎵 72 🎵 73 Exit for Freedom

full band   minus bass

Billy B. Badd

☞ **Bravo! Encore!!**
Remember to practice often and always try to learn more about your instrument.

WAIT! DON'T GO YET!

Even though we hope (and expect) that you will review this entire book again and again, we thought you might like a "cheat sheet," referencing all the notes you learned. Well, happy birthday!

Notes on the bass:

"Where do I go now?"

Here are some suggestions to help you continue to master the bass:

 Repetition is the best way to learn. Review the exercises in this book again and again until all the notes and chords are easily playable without even thinking about them.

 Buy "Bass: Book 2," which teaches many more notes, techniques, and music fundamentals.

 Buy "Bass: Songbook," an excellent book of classic tunes by The Beatles, Clapton, Hendrix, Elton John, and more!

 Enjoy what you do. Whether it's practicing, riffing, jamming, or even cleaning your bass, do it with a smile on your face. Life's too short.

See you next time...

SONG INDEX
(...what book would be complete without one?)